Introduction to Health and Safety Management

Simon Valles and Ian Howlett

Safety Agenda

Copyright Notice

Published by Safety Agenda Ltd 2012.

Copyright © 2012 Safety Agenda Ltd.

First published in London, Great Britain, in 2012.
ISBN: 978-1-4710-3833-4

This book is available at quantity discounts for bulk
purchases.

WARNING!

Be aware! You may hear the phrase "Health and Safety" as a mantra, but it is only worthy of remark in this form before you have a basic understanding of Health and Safety management.

Health and safety is not a doctrine; it is not something you "believe in". Successful health, safety, environmental and quality management is a case of skilled and experienced people looking at the task in hand and deciding on the best way to do it.

It should be inevitable that the best way to do a job is also the safest.

In its most basic form health and safety can make sure you comply with the law, and may mean your company can avoid paying out claims for significant damage or injury.

When fully utilised it will allow you to connect and communicate with your employees in a unique and highly efficient manner. They will get more from you and, in return, you will get more from them.

Safe working is a minimum standard. Unsafe working will measurably hurt your productivity: it will cost you time and money.

Table of Contents

Chapter 1

Introduction

Who is this book for?

This book is an introduction to health and safety management in the construction industry, and the English laws that govern it.

This book is for managers and workers within the construction industry who require a short, readable introduction written in plain English.

What is this book for?

This book can be used for:

- Individual reference

- A reference for a one day supervisors/managers induction or refresher course

- A revision aid for those preparing for the assessment part of the IOSH managing safely course.

Why do we need to know about managing health and safety?

There are four main reasons to improve the way we manage health and safety:

ETHICAL, or moral reasons. Ineffective health and safety management endangers the welfare of other people, including both employees and service users.

ECONOMIC, or financial reasons. Accidents cost companies vast amounts of time and money. Costs could include: time off work; recruiting, training and re-training costs; and loss of reputation.

LEGAL COSTS. These might be fines or compensation costs, but for serious accidents it is increasingly likely that managers and directors will face prison sentences when they are found to have broken Health and Safety laws and regulations.

CONTINUAL IMPROVEMENT. Safer methods of working lead to increases in the value of what is produced, when correctly applied.

With the above in mind it makes sense that we should all have at least a basic knowledge of health and safety management.

Chapter 2

Health and Safety Legislation

Civil and criminal law

There are two branches of English law that we need to consider regarding health and safety at work:

- Civil Law (or common law)

- Criminal Law

Civil law essentially deals with one party attempting to obtain compensation from another party for damage, loss or injury caused due to a breach of duty of care. Decisions are made in court on the basis of precedent (judgements made in previous cases) and "balance of probability" (what is most likely).

Criminal law is based on acts of parliament. Those convicted are punished by prison sentence or fines rather than expected to pay compensation. The burden of proof is higher: "beyond reasonable doubt" rather than "balance of probability".

In cases where a criminal act causes loss or damage, a company will sometimes use a criminal conviction as the basis of a civil case against the guilty party.

It is vital to remember that, unlike most other types of criminal proceedings, when being prosecuted under health and safety law the defendant must prove his or her innocence, rather than the prosecution having prove guilt.

When it comes to Health and Safety law, a defendant is effectively guilty until proven innocent.

Health and Safety at Work Act 1974 (HASAWA or HSWA):

Covers:

- All work activities undertaken
- All those who may be affected by work activities

Employer duties include:

- Risk assessment of potentially hazardous work activities and locations
- Ensuring implementation of control measures identified by risk assessment
- Co-operating with all parties affected by work activities on matters of health and safety
- Arranging and maintaining emergency procedures

Employee duties include:

- Ensuring reasonable care is taken with respect to the health and safety of themselves and those potentially affected by their work. This takes in to account both actions and omissions committed whilst at work. For example, if you switch something on and it causes an accident, that is an action; if you forget to turn something off and it causes an accident, that is an omission

- Cooperating with their employers and co-workers on matters of health and safety

- Using work items and work equipment in a safe manner, as per instruction, training, specified function and design. This includes personal protective equipment (PPE).

- Not misusing, interfering with or modifying any work equipment, tool or installation intended for health, safety or welfare purposes.

All these duties are qualified by the principle of "**so far as is reasonably practicable**".

In other words, measures to reduce risk need not be taken if the monetary cost, time or labour (or other cost) of implementing such measures would be grossly disproportionate to the associated risk.

Chapter 3

What is a Hazard?

Hazards are the basis of risk assessment.

A hazard is defined as anything in the work environment that has the potential to cause harm or damage.

Examples include road traffic; lone working; hazardous chemicals; and working in confined spaces.

We need a method of assessing the risk caused by hazards like these before we can attempt to control them and make the workplace safer. That is what we will now go on to look at.

Chapter 4

A Risk Hierarchy: ERIC

When assessing a risk we have to ask ourselves a number of questions before deciding upon an appropriate Risk Control System (RCS).

An example risk hierarchy is explained below and can be summarised by the acronym ERIC:

E   Eliminate the hazard:

Can we remove the hazard altogether?

This might mean turning off the supply of electricity when working with buried plant (items buried underground such as cables and pipes). In the real world this is unlikely to happen, so we have to look at the next step.

R   Reduce the hazard:

Can we make something less hazardous?

We cannot usually reduce the current flowing in buried plant for the same practical reasons that we can't eliminate it. However, looking at another example, we do tend to reduce electrical hazards due to work equipment by running them at a lower voltage (110V) and selecting equipment that is centrally earthed.

I   Isolate the hazard:

Can we keep the hazard away from people?

Insulating electric cables is an example of isolating the hazard, but going back to our buried plant, it is not practical to try to isolate un-exposed electric cables, especially when you are not quite sure where they are. However, placing split sleeves around exposed live cables, to protect the worker from accidentally coming into contact with the live cable, or protecting the cable from damage is an example of isolating the hazard.

C   Control the hazard:

If we can't do anything else, how can we minimise risk?

This should be considered the last resort, only to be used when the other three options are impracticable. In our buried plant example we can only control the hazard. We can use cable drawings, cable location equipment, personal protective equipment (PPE) and competent staff to control the risk. Because we are all familiar with the risks of buried plant it is easy for us to see that 'C' is the relevant part of the risk hierarchy for this problem. However, it is important to understand the process by which we have arrived at this conclusion.

Chapter 5

Risk Assessment

A risk assessment is a formalised method of looking at hazardous situations in the work place and deciding how best to reduce the associated dangers.

We will need **written records** of our risk assessments at work but it is worth remembering that we all perform dozens of risk assessments every day, it's just that we don't write them down.

Here are three examples in our everyday lives: crossing the street on foot, turning into a road whilst driving, and deciding if a cup of tea or coffee is cool enough to drink. In all these situations we assess the risks involved before proceeding, but in the work place we need a way of writing this down so it is easy for those carrying out the activity to understand what hazards they may encounter and what measures to take.

Measuring risk

There are many ways of quantifying the level of risk that specific hazards pose. The simplest way is to rate hazards as "high", "medium" or "low" risk. This has the disadvantage of being open to interpretation.

A slightly less arbitrary method is described below. Using this method we split risk into two parts, likelihood and severity

RISK = SEVERITY x LIKELIHOOD

We say that the risk from a hazardous situation or procedure is equal to the severity of the damage caused by any accident involving the hazard we are assessing multiplied by the likelihood of an accident occurring due to the hazard in question.

We will look at how to describe severity and likelihood, and then look at some examples.

We can calculate the risk rating for any hazard by assigning number values to the severity and likelihood, usually from 1 to 5 for each. So a 1 for severity might mean that someone just gets a bruised finger if an accident happens, and 5 would mean death or major injury.

Similarly, for likelihood, a 1 would be very unlikely and a 5 would mean almost certain to happen.

Now for an example. Table 1, overleaf, shows a typical layout of a workplace risk assessment, in this case assessing the risk of contracting Weil's disease whilst working on a construction site. Weil's disease, pronounced "Vile's disease" and also known as Leptospirosis, can be caught if a worker comes into contact with rat's urine or the urine of dairy cattle. The initial symptoms are similar to those of flu but the disease progresses to cause both liver and kidney failure, and eventually death, if left untreated.

The different parts of the risk assessment are labelled 1-9 and can be identified as follows:

1. **TITLE**: The title of this risk assessment document.

2. **ACTIVITY**: The work activity being assessed for risk, in this case construction work.

3. **HAZARDS**: Here we identify the hazards associated with the work activity. Obviously there are more hazards affecting construction workers but for the moment we are only going to consider the risk of contracting Weil's disease.

4. **WHO IS AFFECTED?**: Which categories of people might be affected by the hazard(s) listed during the course of the work activity?

5. **INITIAL RISK**: What is the initial risk before we have put any control measures in place? This is calculated using the formula RISK=LIKELIHOOD x SEVERITY. (We can abbreviate Likelihood to LK and Severity to SV.)

6. **CONTROL MEASURES**: What control measures can we put in place to reduce the level of risk from the hazards previously identified (in this case hazards from Weil's disease)?

7. **RESIDUAL RISK**: What risk is still remaining? Using the same method as in box (5) we have to calculate the risk rating after the control measures listed in box (6) have been implemented.

8. **ISSUE DATE/REVIEW DATE**: We need to record when the risk assessment was carried out so that if anything about the work activity has changed, anyone using it will know if the assessment is still valid. A review date must be scheduled for a more thorough check at an agreed date in the future.

9. **RESPONSIBLE PERSON**: A competent (appropriately qualified) person should be assigned to ensure the listed control measures are applied and maintained.

(1) RISK ASSESSMENT FOR WEIL'S DISEASE (LEPTOSPIROSIS)				(5) Initial Risk			(6) CONTROL MEASURES	(7) Residual Risk		
(2) Activity	(3) Hazard	(4) Who is affected?		LK	SV	Risk		LK	SV	Risk
Work near running water or in the presence of rats or dairy cattle	Infection with Weil's disease	Operatives		2	5	10	Information and training			
							Issue of green cards and notification letters to the workers' GPs (doctors).	1	3	3
							Use of personal protective equipment (PPE)			
							Wash hands before eating or smoking			
							Cover all cuts and abrasions			
(9) Responsible Person: Supervisor/Agent							Date issued: 01/04/2012 Review date: 31/03/2013 (8)			

Figure 1: Example of a risk assessment for the risk of contracting weil's disease.

To become comfortable with risk assessment you should choose some of the activities in your own workplace and practice producing risk assessments for them until you feel confident.

REMEMBER: a risk assessment is just a formal way of writing down things you already know about your job, so don't be intimidated!

Also, note that there are many different formats a written risk assessment can take. The example above is only one of many different ways of presenting the information.

Whatever form your risk assessments take the most important thing is to make sure the information it contains is accurate, relevant and easily understood. It is all very well that we produce safety information but it is not going to help anyone if we are the only ones that can understand it!

To summarise, here are five steps to successfully completing a risk assessment:

1. What are the hazards?

2. Who is affected?

3. Evaluate the hazards

4. Decide on control measures

5. Set a review date

Chapter 6

HS(G) 65
Successful
Management of
Health and Safety

Introduction to HSE Guidance Notes

The Health and Safety Executive (HSE) produce guidance notes on many different work activities. These cover a wide range of subjects, ranging from how to safely carry out excavations to safe use of display screen equipment. These documents provide us with information on how to meet the minimum standards necessary to comply with the relevant regulations and legislation.

You are within your rights to ignore guidance notes but bear in mind that if you were to be investigated by the HSE you, as an employer, would have to prove that your way of working was of an equal or higher standard than that prescribed by the guidance note (it is highly unlikely that you would succeed in doing this).

Consequently, we tend to use the advice given to us in the relevant guidance notes, rather than work things out from scratch ourselves. We have paid our taxes which have, in turn, paid for the production of guidance notes, so we might as well use them. They are likely to help us avoid accidents if used correctly.

An important guidance note: HS(G) 65

An important guidance note is
HS(G) 65: Successful management of health and safety.

Its core principals have their origins in quality management. (If you have heard of the Deming cycle, this is one approach to quality management).

It makes sense to consider health and safety management in terms of quality policy, as your customers are unlikely to be satisfied if they become aware they are trading with a company with a poor health and safety record. Also it is likely that poor management of health and safety would adversely affect the cost and quality of your product.

Remember: the costs of not managing health and safety are far greater than the costs of managing it successfully.

So what we need is a process by which we can measure, control and improve the way we manage health and safety. We also need to identify the activities that contribute to health and safety management and determine where they fit in our process.

Luckily, this has already been done for us. Figure 1 shows the HS (G) 65 flowchart, followed by an explanation of each element.

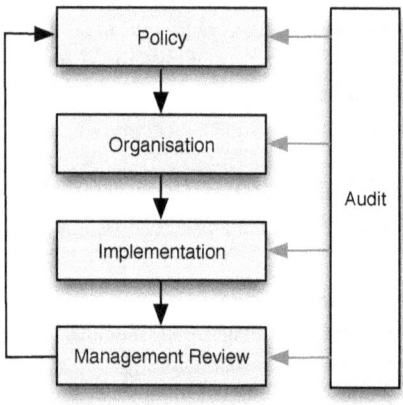

Figure 2. This flow chart represents continual improvement in health and safety management. It is taken from HS(G) 65.

Policy

Successful management of health and safety in the workplace must begin at the top of any organisation. It must be accepted that all workplace situations can be controlled in order to prevent accidents. Policy often outlines a commitment to continual improvement.

An organisation's health and safety policy is used to communicate its broad intentions regarding health and safety at work.

Organisation

Essentially, this section establishes who does what and who is responsible for which actions or duties. There are four fundamental features of this aspect of the system, commonly known as the 4 C's. These are: Competency, Control, Communication and Co-operation. Let us now look at each in more detail.

Competency

There are three main criteria contributing to a worker's competence for a certain task or tasks:

- **Experience**: does the person have a working knowledge of current best practice for the job they are doing? Have they gained enough knowledge and skill from previously doing the job to be able to perform the task safely?

- **Training**: Has the worker completed sufficient training (relevant to the job) in order that they can perform the task without endangering themselves or others?

- **Other qualities**: Are other qualities needed for the job or task? These might include attributes such as physical strength or fitness, a calm personality or the ability to concentrate for long periods of time.

Control

In effect this means management control and management taking responsibility. Again it is a matter of knowing who should be doing what, and ensuring that safe working practices are used.

The initial commitment to managing health and safety must come from top management. They must then guarantee that line managers and other responsible workers control the factors of work which may cause harm. For example, this includes making sure that all the control measures written in the risk assessment are implemented and maintained.

Communication

It is vital that information relevant to health and safety is widely available and easily understood. There is very little point in employers having a safety management system if no one else in the company knows why it is there or what it means.

It needs to be made clear to all employees that management is leading the way in taking responsibility for health and safety, and why health and safety is everyone's responsibility.

Examples of communication might include toolbox talks, safety alerts and safety meetings.

Co-operation

Effective management of health and safety can only occur when everybody participates and everyone involved has a sense of attempting to achieve a common goal.

Planning and Implementation

If the "Organisation" section of our safety management system is basically telling us who is (or should be) doing what, then the "Planning and Implementation" section tells us how they will be doing it. This is where performance standards will be set.

This section may include, for example, carrying out risk assessments and implementing their findings.

Monitoring

There are two types of monitoring we need to consider:

Pro-active monitoring consists of measurements taken before an accident has occurred.

Re-active monitoring consists of measurements taken after an accident or incident has occurred.

Here are some examples of what is included in each type of monitoring:

Proactive Monitoring methods include:

- Health surveillance

- Work place inspections

- Checks on maintenance programs

- Observing Key Performance Indicators (KPIs)

Reactive monitoring methods include:

- Accident/incident reports

- Accident investigations

- Near-miss or hazard reports

- Records of injury or ill-health

AUDIT

The audit is a thorough and systematic examination. It takes in all the available and relevant data for each section of the health and safety management system shown in this flowchart.

This information is then used as evidence to help determine what actions need to be taken at all levels of the organisation in order to improve health and safety at work.

MANAGEMENT REVIEW

At this stage all the information collected and prepared in the previous stages is used to make decisions on how best to improve the health and safety management system.

Improved ways of planning and implementation, and organisation, should be agreed upon at this stage of the process. Performance targets can then be updated.

Chapter 7

The Hidden Costs of Poor Health and Safety Management

It is a grave misconception to consider the provision of health and safety management as a working overhead.

Health and safety management is not just a cost of doing business.

Good health and safety management should be considered a significant part of any organisation's core competency. (The core competency is the thing that an organisation does best.)

Serious accidents can cripple organisations with costs, compensation claims, lost time, and catastrophic loss of reputation. Avoiding accidents should be your first consideration when attempting to avoid going out of business!

Mismanagement of health and safety is a gamble with the odds heavily stacked against you. It is a gamble that has lives and livelihoods at stake. Even minor deviations from best practice can eventually become compounded, with one problem building on top of another, until this directly or indirectly results in an accident or contributes to an unbalanced culture of work. The consequences can be far, far worse than you might expect as a result of the initial mistake.

Uninsured costs

Uninsured costs are costs that your company's insurance policy will not cover, and that your company will have to pay for itself. These costs can be crippling.

Uninsured costs include:

- Lost time

- Extra wages, overtime payments

- Sick pay

- Production delays

- Fines and/or prison sentences

- Loss of contracts

- Loss of reputation

- Legal costs

- Damage to plant, equipment, materials and produce

HSE estimates of accident costs

The HSE has a useful overview of accident costs, at http://www.hse.gov.uk/costs/costs_overview/costs_overview.asp

The HSE estimates that the cost of accidents in construction can account for 3%-6% of total project costs. To put this into perspective, a 5% cost means that a £20m contract would lose £1m on the cost of accidents!

HSE studies also found that uninsured costs can be between 8 and 36 times the cost of an insurance premium paid. This means that for every £1 a company paid in insurance premiums, they had to meet a further £8 to £36 themselves for losses arising from accidents. So if you are paying £10,000 in insurance premiums you may still incur losses of up to £360,000!

Conclusion

The only real insurance against the costs of accidents is to work safely.

To illustrate this point for yourself, think about the last accident experienced by your organisation. As an exercise, make an estimate of the uninsured costs arose as a result.

Chapter 8

Work Equipment and Lifting: PUWER and LOLER

Health and Safety management regarding the use of equipment used in work activities is the subject of two sets of regulations:

- The Provision and use of Work Equipment Regulations (PUWER) 1998

- The Lifting Operations and Lifting Equipment Regulations (LOLER) 1998.

The fundamental principles here can be summed up as:

- "Use the right tool for the right job."

- "Look after your tools and your tools will look after you."

It must also be remembered that work equipment should only be used by competent persons, and that adequate supervision should be provided when deemed necessary by a risk assessment.

Work equipment

Work equipment is governed by The Provision and use of Work Equipment Regulations (PUWER) 1998.

Work equipment is any equipment or installation used by employees at work.

Hired equipment is included in the definition, but not equipment used by the public.

Examples of work equipment include:

- Manually powered tools

- Mechanically powered tools

- Mobile work equipment

- Power presses

- Vending machines (when used by employees)

Risk is controlled by both "hardware" measures (e.g. machine guards) and "software" measures (management procedures).

Work equipment must be:

- Suitable for the task for which it is intended

- Adequately maintained and inspected

- Used correctly: those who use it must have correct and up-to-date information, instruction and training

- Used in conjunction with suitable safety measures (warning signs, isolation from sources of energy, etc)

Work equipment must also conform to the relevant European or British standard, whichever is higher.

Inspection and maintenance regimes should be designed to take into account which parts of the equipment are likely to cause damage should they become faulty, and which parts are difficult to visually inspect without dismantling the piece of equipment.

Lifting operations and lifting equipment

Lifting operations and lifting equipment are governed by The Lifting Operations and Lifting Equipment Regulations (LOLER) 1998. This law applies to both lifting equipment and lifting accessories, that is to say any equipment used at work for lifting or lowering loads.

Examples of lifting equipment:

- Cranes

- Fork-lift trucks

- Hoists

- Mobile elevated work platforms (MEWPs, "cherry pickers")

Escalators are not covered by LOLER; they are covered by more specific legislation.

Examples of lifting accessories:

- Chains

- Slings

- Strops

- Eye bolts

Safety Agenda

Lifts must be:

- Planned and organised by competent people

- Supervised by competent people

- Carried out by competent people

- Carried out in a safe manner

Lifting equipment/accessories must be:

- Marked to indicate the safe working load

- Positioned on stable ground

- Positioned or installed to minimise any risks identified

- Examined or inspected by competent people

- Thoroughly examined before first use

- Inspected prior to each subsequent use

Lifting equipment and accessories used for carrying people must be thoroughly examined at least every 6 months.

All other lifting equipment must be thoroughly examined at least every 12 months.

Examination reports must be submitted to the employer.

Chapter 9

Personal Protective Equipment (PPE)

Personal protective equipment (PPE) is equipment worn or used by an individual to reduce the risk of an accident occurring due to a specified hazard.

Examples of PPE include:

- High visibility clothing, such as "high-vis" vests

- Protective gloves

- Safety helmets

- Lanyard and harness

- Breathing apparatus

- Protective eye-wear

In risk hierarchy of ERIC that we covered in chapter 4, we said that PPE is a control measure or risk control system. This means that it comes under the "Control" section of ERIC, and should be considered as a last resort when trying to construct a safe system of working.

This may seem counter-intuitive, and not be what you would expect, but using the ERIC risk hierarchy you should only consider using PPE when control measures that Eliminate, Reduce or Isolate a person affected from a hazard have been judged inadequate.

Some companies, however, set minimum standards of PPE use throughout their workplaces (e.g. hi-vis vest, safety helmet, safety eyewear and gloves); although this approach encourages conformity it can sometimes distract from task-specific PPE requirements. In other words, if you are wearing standard safety eyewear but need to change to eyewear with a higher level of protection for a particular task, you may forget or be reluctant to do so.

When choosing and employing PPE take the following into account:

- Is the item of PPE suitable for the job it is being asked to do?

- Is the item of PPE being used correctly?

- Does the chosen item of PPE actually reduce the specified risk to the user whilst working?

- PPE must be regularly maintained and monitored for defects.

- Correct and relevant information and training must be given and available to the user.

- PPE must conform to the relevant British or European manufacturing standard.

Employers have a duty to provide PPE free of charge whenever it is required.

Circumstances in which PPE is required will be determined by risk assessment.

Chapter 10

Manual Handling

Manual handling is governed by the Manual Handling Operations Regulations 1992 (as amended) (MHOR).

A manual handling operation is defined as "any transporting or supporting of a load (including the lifting, putting down, pushing, pulling, carrying or moving thereof) by hand or bodily force".

This includes operations such as:

- Lifting work equipment out of a van

- Moving office furniture

- Carrying box files

- Moving or setting up safety barriers or fencing

- Pushing or pulling wheeled objects (e.g. a trolley)

Incorrect manual handling technique frequently leads to work related upper limb disorders (WRULDs) and back pain. Of all the injuries that cause the injured person to be off work for more than three days, 1 in 3 are due to manual handling.

In the risk hierarchy of ERIC that we covered in chapter 4, we can see that before beginning any manual handling operation we should consider, among other things, the following:

- Can the lift be automated?

- Can the lift be mechanised?

- Is it a two-person job?

- Can lighter components or materials be specified?

- Is PPE required (e.g. gloves)?

- Can items to be manually handled be labelled with their accurate weights?

The key point is that before the activity begins all foreseeable hazards or likely changes in conditions should have been taken into account.

When assessing the risk attributable to the operation, you should bear in mind the following:

Load: is the load heavy, bulky, difficult to hold on to, unstable, sharp, slippery?

Individual: consider the age, gender, fitness, strength, training etc of the worker.

Task: how does the nature of the task affect the person doing the job?

Environment: how do lighting, ventilation or obstacles affect the job?

Chapter 11

Slips, Trips and Falls

Slips, trips and falls are accidents involving individuals losing control of their own movement during un-aided transit, resulting in unrestrained motion in the direction of the ground or other surface.

The causes of such accidents are often features of the work place environment. Examples include:

- Uneven ground

- Untidy workplace

- Wet surfaces

Causes relating to the individual and the use of equipment include:

- Carrying a load along an unplanned route

- Worn-out or damaged footwear

- Poor knowledge or lack of experience of the workplace

Slips, trips and falls account for over a third of work place accidents.

Vigilance is required to check for:

- Spillage of liquids

- Trailing cables

- Poor storage of equipment and materials,

- Obstructions caused by rubbish

- Poorly secured rugs, mats or carpets

- Poor lighting

It may often be the case that a slip/trip/fall hazard is avoided due to an individual's own awareness or physical dexterity. However, companies must have a reporting procedure for such occurrences in order to help prevent future accidents.

Chapter 12

Electrical Hazards

Electrical current is hazardous. The two most significant risks associated with electricity are:

- **Physical contact** when people or objects touch the electrical current

- **Fire ignition source** where the electricity starts a fire.

The physical effects of electric current on the human body include burns and heart attacks. On average, in the UK 1000 accidents involving electricity are reported each year, with around 30 fatalities. Most of these fatalities are caused by contact with underground equipment and overhead cables.

When working near overhead cables the first thing that needs to be carried out is a site-specific risk assessment. Take account of the following:

- Height of overhead cables

- Type of cable (e.g. telecommunications, electricity supply)

- Amount of current carried by each cable identified

- Maximum height of any equipment you are planning to use

- The competence of the people who will be doing the work

- Should "goal posts" and bunting be erected

- Can the cables be thrown dead (where any current is switched off) for the duration of your operation?

Don't take risks with electrical current: always plan ahead.

When excavating near to underground/sub-surface equipment carrying electrical current, you must ensure that:

- A site-specific risk assessment has been carried out

- Operatives have been briefed with the risk assessment

- Accurate and readable cable plans are available and on-site

- The work area has been thoroughly surveyed

- Cable location equipment is used, for example ground penetrating radar or radio detection

Electrical installations should be subject to a program of maintenance. New installations should be designed and installed to the specifications of an applicable standard such as BS7671.

Operating voltages should be reduced when it is practical to do so. The use of safety devices that detect electrical faults (e.g. Residual Current Devices, RCDs) should be considered.

Damaged or suspect equipment should be taken out of use and quarantined so that nobody else can use it. This includes equipment or leads with exposed or damaged wiring.

Workers using electrical equipment must be trained and competent.

PAT Testing

Electrical equipment such as drills, extension leads and computers should be maintained as per PUWER '98, and PAT (Portable Apparatus Test) tested.

Chapter 13

Fire Hazards

The effects of fire in the work place can be devastating, both in financial terms and in human loss or injury. Some firms that are seriously affected by fire never fully recover from the disruption and cost.

Regulatory Reform (Fire Safety) Order 2005

The Regulatory Reform (Fire Safety) Order 2005 sets out certain measures we are legally obliged to have in place in order to reduce as far as possible the risks related to fire. They can be summarised as follows:

Employers and landlords must ensure:

- Adequate means of raising alarm
- Adequate means of escape
- Adequate means of fighting a fire
- Adequate emergency lighting
- Adequate maintenance of fire protection systems
- Adequate instruction, information and training
- A fire risk assessment is carried out

The definition of "adequate" will vary from site to site and will depend on the findings of a fire risk assessment.

Classes of fire

Different types of fire can be classified by fuel type. In the UK these classifications are as follows:

Class A: cloth, paper wood, etc

Class B: flammable liquids (e.g. fuel oil)

Class C: flammable gasses (e.g. propane)

Class D: metals such as magnesium or aluminium

Class E: Electrical fires

Class F: cooking oils or fats

Fire extinguishers

New fire extinguishers should have a red-coloured body with a different coloured patch, no larger than 10% of the total surface area, to show which type of fire extinguisher it is. Table 2 shows which kind of fire extinguisher to use on different types of fire and what colour the label will be.

Colour of label	Type of extinguisher	Class of fire					
		A	B	C	D	Electrical	F
Red	Water	✔					
Black	Carbon Dioxide	✔	✔	✔		✔	
Cream	Foam	✔	✔				
Blue	Powder	✔	✔	✔	✔	✔	
Yellow	Wet chemical	✔					✔

Figure 3: Types of fire extinguisher and their uses.

Chapter 14

Safety Signs

Safety signs are an important communication tool. They have two main purposes:

1. Alerting workers and members of the public to hazards they may face

2. Giving information on controls that are in place to keep them safe.

When using safety signs consider the following:

- Is the sign the correct size to be seen clearly by the intended viewer?

- Is the sign placed so that the view of it is not obscured?

- Is there any movement-based change that might obscure the sign (e.g. if a sign is attached to a gate or door, will the sign still be visible if the door or gate is left open)?

- Does the sign need to be illuminated?

Also bear in mind that:

- Safety signs must be maintained

- Complex signs must be explained

- Road traffic signs must be used to control traffic where deemed necessary

The need for safety signs should be determined by a risk assessment.

In addition to diagrams, different colour, shape and pattern codes are used to indicate the type of message the sign is designed to convey. Some examples are given below:

Red on White: Prohibition.
This sign tells you something you must not do in the affected area.

Black on Yellow: Hazard.
This sign indicates there is a specific hazard near the location of the sign.

Hazardous areas may be marked out using this yellow and black striped pattern.

White on Green: Safe Condition.
An indication of something provided to ensure safety, for example the direction of a fire exit

Blue on white: Mandatory.
Indicates something you must do, such as wear a specific type of PPE.

Chapter 15

Hazardous Substances: COSHH

It is important to be aware of hazardous substances in the workplace. We need to identify which hazardous substances we store, transport or use during the course of the work activities we are responsible for. We also need to know who might be affected by exposure to these substances, the extent of any likely exposure (duration, dose and frequency) and the possible long and short term effects of exposure.

The Control of Substances Hazardous to Health regulations (COSHH) govern how we treat hazardous substances in the work place.

The main things to consider when managing the use and storage of hazardous substances are:

- What have we got?

- What could it do?

- Who could it hurt?

Once these questions have been answered accurately, suitable safeguards can be selected and implemented.

COSHH regulations apply to:

- Chemicals (encountered in liquid, solution, particulate suspension or emulsion form)

- Dusts

- Fumes

When determining control measures you need to consider:

- The type of damage that may be caused

- How much contact with eyes or skin might occur and how much may be ingested

- The size of the area of the body that may be exposed

Different types of control include:

- Segregation: keeping away from the substance)

- Identification and labelling

- General ventilation

- Engineering control (e.g. local exhaust ventilation)

- Containment: keeping the substance within a controlled area

Employees must be made aware of which substances they are likely to come into contact with during the course of work activity, their possible effects and what controls have been selected to protect those who might be affected by them.

You should ensure employees are aware of the COSHH data regarding any hazardous substance they may encounter or use whilst at work.

Below are some hazard symbols that you should be familiar with. COSHH requires that these symbols are visible on all chemical substances that carry these risks.

Chapter 16

Display Screen
Equipment (DSE)

Display Screen Equipment, or DSE, is equipment used for viewing information.

DSE includes: Cathode Ray Tube (CRT) displays, such as older televisions and computer screens, and newer flatscreen displays, such as those found on almost all modern computers.

DSE does not include: mobile computer systems (or those on board vehicles) or those for public use; projected film, television, videos and DVDs; cash registers; calculators; or typewriters.

The "user" of DSE is defined as someone who, whilst at work:

- Uses DSE almost continuously on most days

- Has no alternative method of work

- Has no choice but to use DSE

- Requires specific training and/or skills

- Has to maintain high concentration levels over time

- Performs high speed data transfer

Users of DSE are at risk of conditions including:

- WRULDs (Work Related Upper Limb Disorders)

- Stress

- Eyestrain

- Back problems

Chapter 17

Accident and Near Miss Reporting

Before we discuss in detail the nature and value of accident and near miss reporting we need to understand what we mean by each term. For our purposes the following definitions are most useful and accurate:

What is an accident?

An **accident** is an unplanned event that **has** caused injury or harm to a person or people or damage to property or the environment.

For example, getting run over by a car, hurting your ear by pushing a pen into it, or exposure to asbestos fibres at work are all examples of accident.

It is important to note that we are talking about accidents and near misses that happen to people who are at work (employees), and happen to other people who may have been affected by others working (members of the public, for example) because this determines if the event is covered by HASWA and its associated regulations. By contrast, we are not concerned here by accidents that do not happen to employees or are not the result of work taking place.

What is a near-miss?

A **near-miss** is an unplanned event that **could have** resulted in injury or harm to a person or people or damage to property or the environment.

Examples of near-misses include nearly getting run over by a car because you were distracted by using your mobile phone, disobeying a warning sign telling you to wear a hard hat in the area you are entering, or using an item of electrical equipment with a damaged power cord.

Pro-active and Reactive measures

One of the key differences between accidents and near-misses is the taking of what are known as "pro-active" and "reactive" measures to prevent accidents occurring in the future. If a near-miss is reported and someone takes measures to prevent re-occurrence that is termed a pro-active measure because it is occurring prior to an accident happening.

Measures taken to prevent accidents reoccurring are termed reactive as they are taken as a reaction to an accident happening.

Why record accidents and near-misses?

There is value in recording information about accidents and near-misses because analysing these reports can help us to put in place measures that could minimise the chances of future incidents.

RIDDOR

Under the **Reporting of Injuries, Diseases and Dangerous Occurrences Regulations 1995 (RIDDOR)** employees and employers have a duty to record and report accidents and near-misses (when they fall within the regulation's schedule of dangerous occurrences), but as ever the regulations are

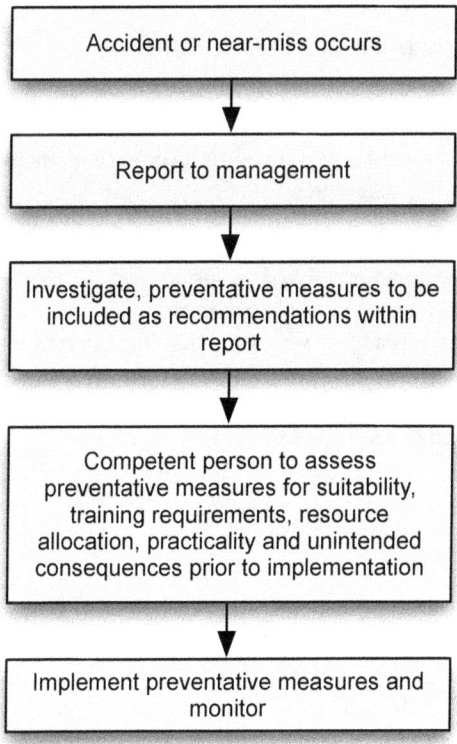

Figure 4: An example diagram of how a company might manage accidents and near-misses:

just there to make sure you are doing something that will benefit your business anyway.

Assessing preventative measures

Assessing preventative measures before putting them in place is an important step because although the measures identified might help prevent one kind of incident they could end up leading to another.

For example, a contractor working on refurbishing a motorway tunnel was asked to install plastic "nappies" on their mobile elevated work platforms to prevent oil leaks damaging the road way without taking into account that the work they were doing would produce sparks and burning embers from the use of oxy/acetylene burning equipment; this resulted in a fire and lost time.

Severity of accidents: the accident pyramid

Accidents can be organised into a pyramid shape to show how often different types of accident occur. This useful diagram was first drawn by HW Heinrich as early as 1931, proving the lasting value of the idea. The figures vary from one industry to another, but in 1969 Frank Bird found that:

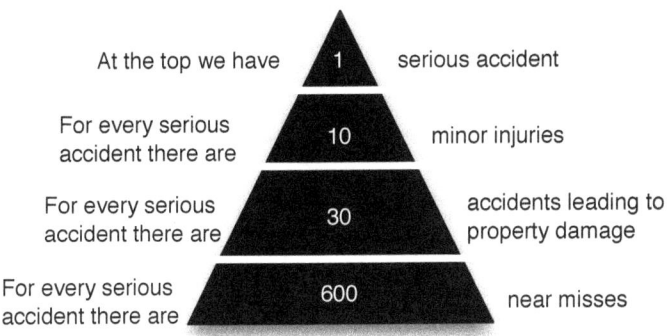

Figure 5: The accident pyramid.

Chapter 18

Continual
Improvement

To understand the value of health and safety management, we have to relate the subject to other aspects of the company. To help us do this, we must first look at some additional ideas.

Safety is desirable

The most basic idea is that when a customer buys a product or service, part of what is being paid for is the safe production of the product. In other words, successful health and safety management is an inherent part of any desirable product or service.

A brief description of some other useful concepts follows.

Utility

Definition of Utility

Utility is just another way of saying how useful something is.

The utility to be gained by a certain activity depends on a wide range of factors and the differing priorities of those affected by the activity. Those affected, who stand to lose or gain if an activity is carried out, are sometimes referred to as stake-holders.

As an example, if the activity is laying a new utility service (gas, water etc) then overall utility increases for the people who have more reliable or safer access to the service, and for those who have financially benefited from the activity of laying a new service. All stake-holders face a reduction in overall utility if workers or property are damaged during the works, or if the work activity itself causes damage to the environment.

The law of diminishing returns

Next we need to consider the law of diminishing returns, which states:

Utility diminishes with each like unit consumed.

In other words, utility decreases each time you do the same thing. This is illustrated in the following example:

Marianne likes Mars bars. Her friend Mick buys her a Mars bar, which she gratefully accepts and consumes. Observing Marianne's pleasure, Mick decides to give her another Mars bar, which is again gratefully received and consumed by Marianne. Although Marianne enjoyed her second Mars bar, she didn't get quite as much enjoyment as she did from the first one.

If Marianne were to consume yet another Mars bar the utility gained would continue to fall.

One might imagine the situation in which Marianne had, for some reason, consumed twelve Mars bars. At some point in this sequence the next Mars bar consumed will be the one that makes Marianne feel unwell. At this point Mars bar consumption results in a net loss in utility.

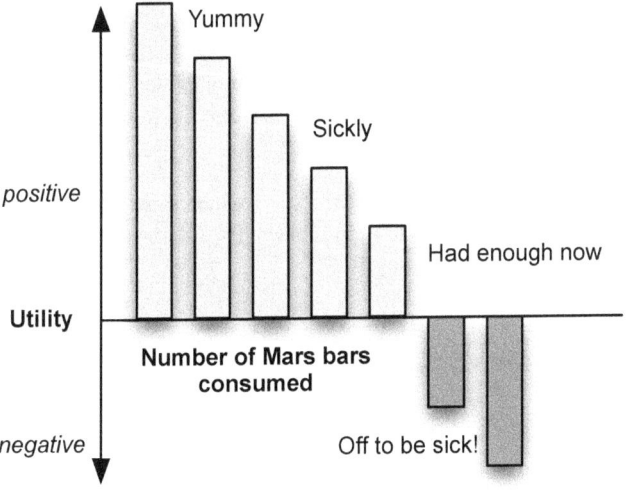

Figure 6: What happens to utility as Marianne consumes additional Mars bars. Utility goes down with each additional Mars bar consumed.

This idea is shown in Figure 6. Here you can see that, although they are related, **utility is not the same as price**. In the example above the cost of each successive Mars bar remains the same but the utility changes with each additional unit consumed.

More trouble than it is worth?

The law of diminishing returns expresses itself in terms of health and safety legislation as the principle of "**as far as is reasonably practicable**", when applied to the time, effort and expense spent on controlling risk.

We can phrase this another way: **when does something become more trouble than it is worth?**

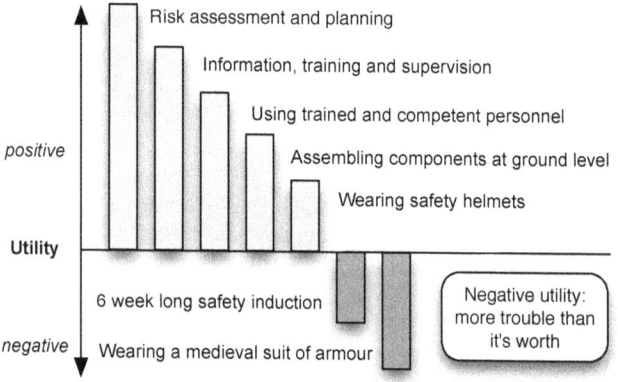

Figure 7: Various measures taken to reduce risk, and the utility of each measure. In this example we are thinking of measures to reduce the risks from working at height.

In Figure 7, we assume a relationship between utility and measures taken to reduce risk. In this example we are referring to measures to reduce the risks from working at height.

Towards the right hand side of the graph the amount of utility gained by implementing a measure drops below zero and becomes negative.

The point at which the utility gained by implementing a measure becomes negative defines whether or not a measure, or set of measures, is reasonably practicable.

Value Chains

We can draw a diagram showing how utility is split among everyone with an interest in a project. This is referred to as a value chain.

The production of manufactured goods or services can also be described in terms of utility. Everyone involved gains a certain degree of utility as a result of their involvement in the enterprise in question. When viewed together, these people and companies form a value chain.

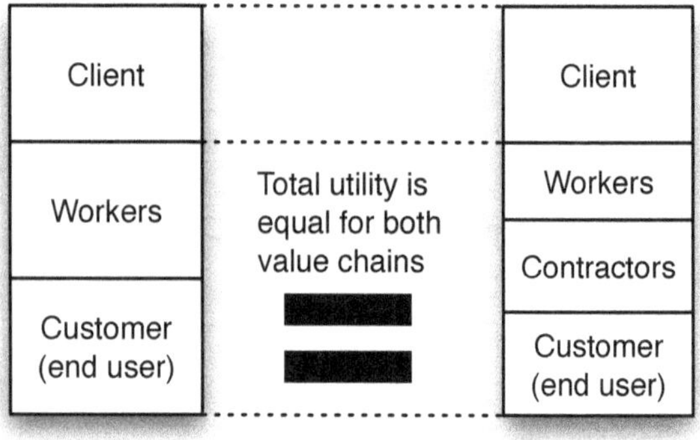

Figure 8: A dysfunctional value chain when the contractors are involved. No additional value is created by the contractors.

Figure 8 shows two examples of a value chain. The value chain on the left represents a situation where a client directly procures and manages the labour (the "workers") necessary to complete its task. It is important to accept that the customer or end user includes everyone that is affected by the product, not just the buyer who signs the cheques.

The value chain on the right represents a situation where the client hires a contractor to procure and manage labour. There are now four parties involved, rather than three. It would appear that in this situation each link in the value chain could expect a reduction in its level of utility. Somebody, it would seem, has to lose.

In reality, Figure 8 describes a dysfunctional client-contractor relationship that is not working properly. The extra layer of management does nothing except reduce the utility of the other stakeholders.

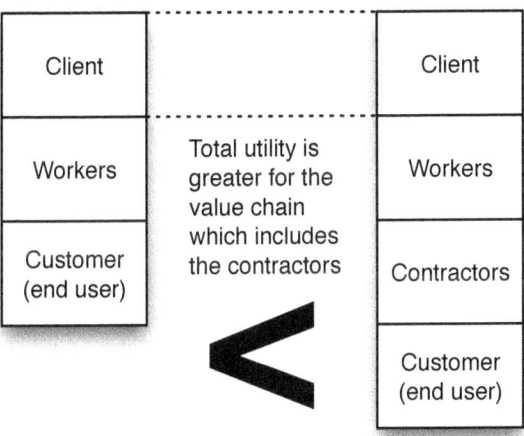

Figure 9: A much better value chain when the contractors are involved. The contractors are creating additional value.

The consequences of such a damaging condition are many, but may include:

- Unsatisfied customers

- Workers and managers under undue pressure and stress

- Reduced standards of product quality

- Reduced standards of Health and Safety

- Reduced standards of environmental care

- Reduced profits

When the quality of the product deteriorates, this reduction in value is reflected back up the chain to the detriment of all other links in the chain. In other words, everyone loses.

Obviously in this case we need to discover and embrace improved methods of working and ways of thinking about work.

By improving things, the temptation for the contractor to just "take his cut" is removed. The responsibility is on the contractor to work more cost effectively and efficiently. This actively generates wealth and increases the overall level of utility in the value chain. This is shown in Figure 8.

The need for continual improvement

How can we achieve the result in the previous diagram? How can we work more effectively? By what process can we seek to continually improve the way we work and what we produce?

The answer is that the number of ways of doing this are too great to list and beyond the scope of this book. Those methods are there, waiting to be discovered and implemented by workers, supervisors, managers and clients.

Increases in efficiency rely primarily on focused and well-informed management and commitment to achievable goals.

The following chapter, on the Deming Cycle, is one way to seek continual improvement in the way we work.

Chapter 19

The Deming Cycle

One way to seek continual improvement is to apply the Deming Cycle when making decisions about work undertaken. This is named after W. Edwards Deming, an American who went to Japan in the 1950s and became widely known for his work on improving product quality.

Here is a brief overview of the Deming Cycle and its parts:

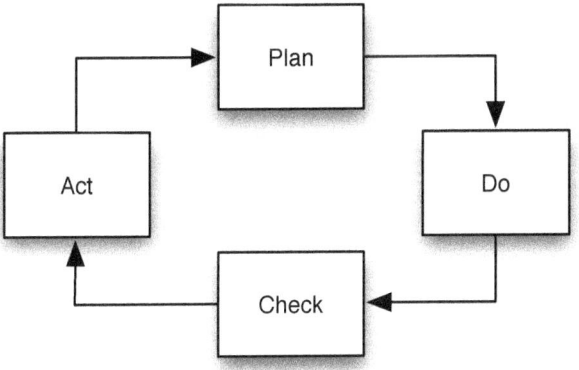

Figure 10: The Deming Cycle for continuous improvement.

Plan the work: find the best way of doing the job

Do the work that has been planned; ensure everyone knows what they should be doing.

Check that the work is going according to plan and record your observations and measurements, with reference to your organisation's values and goals.

Act. Make informed decisions on adjustment of work activities according to your findings.

Using the Deming cycle in management procedure is a basic requirement (and the foundation) of international standards including **ISO 9001: Quality Management, ISO 14001: Environmental Management and OHSAS 18001: Occupational Health and Safety**.

Always strive to have the most relevant and accurate information available to you and your employees. Allow time and space for your employees to give you as much useful information as you give them, and provide the opportunity for this information to be successfully used.

Chapter 20

Negotiating Change

In many cases, despite all the measures and systems that may be in place, many organisations fail to achieve continual improvement in health and safety performance.

This should come as no surprise in established industries, where certain attitudes and working practices are deeply ingrained in the culture of an organisation.

We will now consider a few methods which help us to actually implement measures to improve health and safety successfully, and with a minimum of resistance.

Three approaches to negotiating change

Firstly, we are going to consider three approaches to changing what people do (hopefully for the better) whilst at work:

1. Change the physical environment

This might include removing unapproved tools from use or preventing the use of certain equipment. This approach will yield observable short-term results. However, the imaginative worker will often find ways around such measures unless a high level of supervision and discipline are applied.

2. Discipline and punitive measures

As in, "if you're caught doing X, it will cost you Y". In this case X is a prohibited activity (e.g. not wearing PPE as prescribed) and Y is the punishment (e.g. loss of bonus payments, written warnings, dismissal). The success of this approach depends on how diligently it is applied. One drawback of this approach is that that the threat of punishment becomes the worker's main reason for complying. This can lead to poor morale and an "us and them" relationship between workers and management, both of which can form barriers to improvement in the longer term. Also, this approach may encourage workers to try to "cover up" mistakes and not report workplace hazards. An unreported hazard is a potential accident.

3. Negotiation, communication and explanation

If someone is expected to change the way they do something (and they may have been doing something a certain way for a very long time) they are more likely to be cooperative if they can see how the changes will benefit them. Changes that improve health and safety are often perceived as detrimental to productivity, and slowing things down. This myth needs to be dispelled (of course, it is only a myth if the measures to be implemented are sensible). Short-term reductions in productivity become insignificant compared to the long term gains for quality, productivity and reputation that high standards of health and safety build up.

In real life a combination of all three of the above approaches is usually needed when implementing change.

Choosing the most effective combination of these approaches is often challenging. Your strategy will depend on any number of factors, which may include:

- Your own strengths and weaknesses

- The level of authority given to you by your employers

- The strengths and weaknesses of those under your supervision

- The type and extent of any changes to be made

Appendix 1

Exam Technique

During your career you are likely to sit exams for your professional qualifications. For many of us, who have not taken exams since leaving school many years ago, this can be daunting.

Firstly, it is important to realise that exam technique is a skill, and you can learn it just like many other skills. A written exam tests two things: can you remember knowledge, and can you show the examiner that you understand the subkect? is not only a test of your ability to remember knowledge. It is also an assessment of your skill at demonstrating your level of understanding of the subject by putting pen to paper.

We will now look at a few tips to help you successfully pass your exams.

Answer The Question!

This may seem obvious but many marks have been lost through misreading the question or ignoring what it is asking for. Read the question slowly, and read it at least two or three times. Answer the question that has actually been asked.

Example question: Which of the following is not part of the risk assessment process?

a)   Identify the hazards

b)   Assess the load

c)   Determine who is affected

d)   Set review date.

Incorrect reading of the question might lead you to think along the lines of "Setting the review date is the final step in the risk assessment process", or "You must assess the load before carrying out manual handling operations".

Although these things are both correct as statements of fact, they are not correct answers to the question that has been set.

The correct answer would be,

"b) Assess the load" is not part of the risk assessment process.

Use past papers from previous exams

By looking at past papers you can get a feel for the way questions are worded and see which topics come up most often. You may find that certain core topics turn up year after year. This could help you decide which parts of the course to spend the most time revising and what type of questions to practice most often.

If you see questions that you cannot yet answer, you know where you might still need to do some work to learn more. Don't worry though: most students come out of most exams thinking that the exam paper they actually sat was a lot easier than the past papers! This is often because the course content has changed slightly, so you have been taught slightly different things to the students who took the previous exams.

Exam papers from previous years may be available from your training provider. If not, you should be able to get them from the internet or other another publisher.

Practice

As we noted above, exam technique is a skill, and as with all skills a certain amount of practice is necessary if you are to improve. You can start easily by just seeing if you can answer a few questions. When you feel confident you know how to answer questions on a certain subject you could even try doing an entire past paper and timing yourself.

Don't panic!

A certain amount of "nervous energy" can be a useful thing but save it for exam day.

If there is part of a subject you are having trouble understanding, or that you do not feel has been explained to you clearly enough, make a note of it and ask your instructor about it next time you are in contact with them. Don't be scared to ask questions: the chances are that if you are not sure about something others in your group will be having the same problem.

Remember that it is easier to learn new information and understand new concepts when you are happy and relaxed. Try to leave any pressures from work life or home life at the training room door.

Pack your bag the night before

Each exam varies, but you usually want to take pens, pencils, erasers and a ruler. Take spares: pens run out, pencils snap, and so on. Take a watch to make sure you keep an eye on the time in the exam room. Remember that mobile phones will most likely not be allowed, so you can't use the clock on your phone!

Conclusion

Following these simple rules should allow you to have a successful and rewarding learning experience.

Good luck!

Appendix 2

Relevant Acts and Regulations

Acts of Parliament

- Health & Safety at Work Act 1974 (known as HASAWA or HSWA).

- Fire Precautions Act 1971

Regulations

Regulations are legally binding, approved by Parliament and usually made under the Health and Safety at Work Act. The following regulations apply to work places in general:

- The Management of Health & Safety at Work Regulations 1999

- The Construction (Design and Management) Regulations 2007

- The Workplace (Health, Safety & Welfare) Regulations 1992

- The Provision & Use of Work Equipment Regulations 1998

- The Manual Handling Operations Regulations 1992

- The Personal Protection Equipment Regulations 1992

- The Health & Safety (Display Screen Equipment) Regulations 1992

- The Control of Asbestos Regulations 2012

Other regulations

- Health & Safety (First Aid) Regulations 1981

- Noise at Work Regulations 2005

- Electricity at Work Regulations 1989

- Electrical Equipment (Safety) Regulations 1994

- Reporting of Injuries, Diseases, Dangerous Occurrences Regulations 1995

- Regulatory Reform (Fire Safety) Order 2005

- Pressure Systems (Safety) Regulations 2000

- Control of Substances Hazardous to Health Regulations 2002

Find legislation on the web

The relevant legislation that you need for your job is on the UK Government's website at http://www.legislation.gov.uk.

This site supercedes previous government legislation websites, and brings everything together in one place.

Appendix 3

Safety Agenda: Powerful Software for the Construction Industry

The authors of this book are co-founders of Safety Agenda Ltd, a UK-based company specialising in software for the construction industry. Our software helps companies to manage their businesses more profitably in areas relating to health and safety, and environmental management.

Please see http://www.safetyagenda.com for a full list of our products and services, or email info@safetyagenda.com. Alternatively, you can call us on 020 7193 0835 for a friendly chat.

At Safety Agenda, our aim is to ensure successful Health and Safety Management becomes an integral part of:

Saving you money: You can avoid costs due to legal action, sick pay, lost time, damage to plant and equipment, loss of contracts and loss of reputation.

Making you money: Major contractors and clients prefer working with companies who have sound management of health and safety. Manage this area well and new business opportunities will arise for you.

Our core principle is that by working safely the costs of accidents are avoided, profitability is maximised and new business opportunities will become available.

Safety performance and legal compliance combine to provide challenges for companies of all sizes.

Through our products and services, Safety Agenda helps customers to find cost-effective and cost-beneficial solutions to these challenges that mean your company won't just cope with business conditions but will thrive in any working environment.

Safety Agenda
Training Manager

Easy-to-use training records management.

Know who is qualified, when qualifications need renewing, and see certificates immediately.

Free trial: http://www.sa-trainingmanager.com

If you're struggling to keep track of your workers, their numerous qualifications, and their expiry dates, then Safety Agenda Training Manager is the product for you.

This easy-to-use, secure, web-based software allows you to track qualifications and training requirements for all your workers. You can also track budgets, so you'll always know what your training costs are.

At the touch of a button, you can produce a full training matrix report, showing who in your company is qualified, which is ideal for winning new business with tenders, where you need to prove your workers' competence. With early warnings of upcoming expiry dates, you can improve your cash flow by never having to turn down or delay work due to a lack of qualified workers.

As enforcement of legislation gets stricter, if qualifications expire and you don't realise, then there's an accident, your company – and you personally – could be in serious trouble.

With this system, you can sleep easy in your bed knowing that everything is under control.

Everything is in one place, so you can say goodbye to multiple spreadsheets and piles of paper. There's no need to waste time checking that everyone has the latest version of your information: everyone just accesses the web site, so you never need to worry about document control again. Plus, we back up all your data, automatically, so you never need to stress over losing your information, or over those backups you never quite get round to doing!

One of the most useful and unique features will save you huge amounts of time on client sites: each worker gets a code, which gives direct access to his list of qualifications, and scanned certificates. When the worker arrives on site and needs to produce his documentation, you can just send an SMS text message directly to his phone, giving a web link that immediately lets the site manager see his documentation so he can begin working straight away.

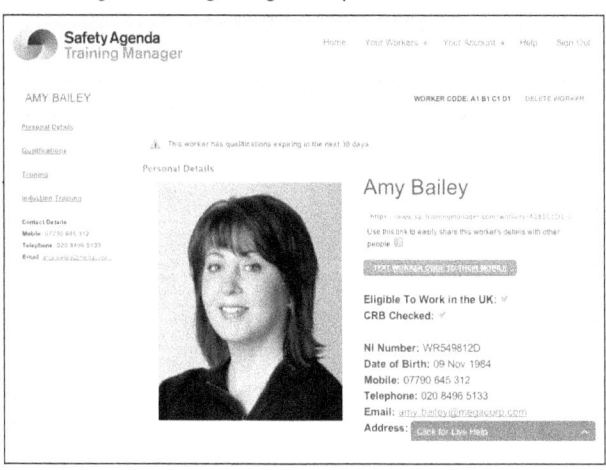

Safety Agenda
Site Waste
Management Plan
Green Check ✓

Easy-to-use Site Waste Management Plans.

The simplest way to stay legal with SWMP 2008 and Waste Duty of Care Regulations.

Free trial: http://www.sa-swmp.com

If your projects generate any kind of waste, then you are legally required to keep a Site Waste Management Plan. Our easy-to-use, secure web-based software leads you step by step through the process, making sure you're always legally compliant, and saving you lots of admin time.

With fixed penalty notices spilling out like parking tickets, and prosecutions possible of up to £50,000 for either a company or an individual – that means YOU – this software gives you everything you need to answer the inspectors with when they come calling.

Plus, you get great reports, at any stage of your project, at the touch of a button, allowing you to manage your projects for greater profit by better handling of waste.

You can share your project with your team, and easily give everyone their own login, so that managers, site staff and admin personnel can all work on the plan without having to worry about version control. We also back up all your data, automatically, so you never need to stress over losing your information, or over those backups that didn't get done just before your computer died!

Everything is mapped to European Waste Codes, and has been fully checked for legal compliance, so you're never left worrying if what you've produced is good enough to avoid the law! If the regulations change, we'll update our software too, free of charge.

By keeping your SWMP on the web, it's always available on site, a key part of the regulations that many people fall foul of.

You can also compare multiple projects quickly and easily, to see how you are performing as an entire company, and identify possible changes in waste handling strategy for the whole company.

Begin your free trial today: go to http://www.sa-swmp.com to see a demonstration video and get started.

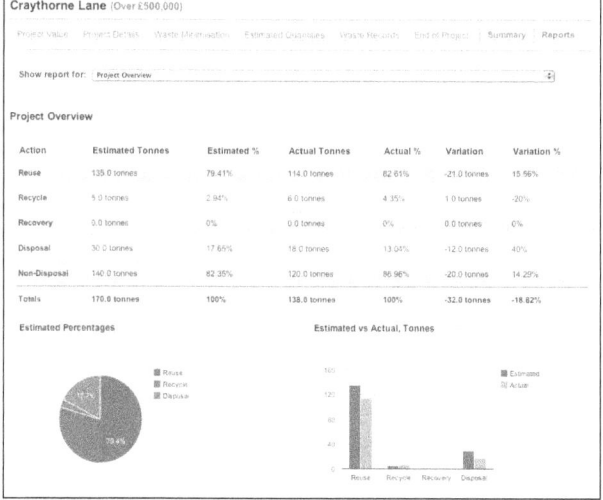

Safety Agenda
Directory

The construction industry directory for health and safety information

The simplest way to stay compliant with Regulation 4 of CDM, checking competence.

Sign up at http://www.sa-directory.com

"No person on whom these Regulations place a duty shall - (a) appoint or engage a CDM co-ordinator, designer, principal contractor or contractor unless he has taken reasonable steps to ensure that the person to be appointed or engaged is competent;"

~ The Construction (Design and Management) Regulations 2007, Regulation 4(1)(a)

If you need a contractor in hurry, you can turn to our directory and find all the information you need to check that their health and safety standards meet your requirements.

If your company is a contractor, you need to be listed here so that you can quickly get new work without having to fill in endless PQQs and tender documents – you can just point your prospective client to your entry on the directory, and they will have all the information they need in a standardised format.

To summarise the benefits of joining the Safety Agenda Directory:

- Get new work from the companies searching our database

- Reduce administrative time and costs of qualifying to work with major contractors and clients

- Demonstrate your competence in managing Health & Safety

- Save time dealing with auditors, PQQs and accreditation bodies: just point them to your listing here

- Get a Safety Agenda certificate for your wall and use the Safety Agenda certification and logo on your promotional material

So if you're a contractor, or you respond to PQQs, you need to be on Safety Agenda Directory. Go to http://www.sa-directory.com and sign up today.

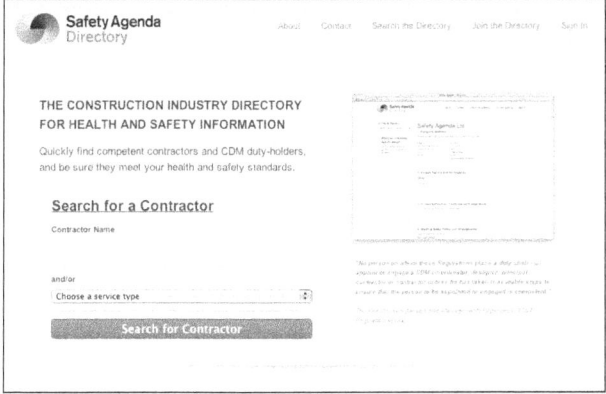

Safety Agenda
Plant and Asset Manager

Easy-to-use plant and asset control system.

Save money by efficiently managing your own equipment and external equipment hiring. Cut costs on every single project you have.

Get in touch with Safety Agenda for more info.

Most construction and demolition companies are losing money every single day by failing to correctly manage one of their most expensive assets: their plant, tools and equipment.

Keeping track of which equipment is allocated to which project can be very difficult, and mistakes can be very costly, as new equipment is needlessly purchased, and equipment is needlessly hired externally.

Without a sophisticated modern computer system to support your plant and asset management, your company is almost certainly losing money, day by day, on every single project you are running.

Safety Agenda Plant and Asset Manager lets you quickly and simply make sure you are making the best use of every single piece of equipment you own.

In day-to-day use, you get to see exactly what equipment you have, where it is, and whether you can fulfil requests for equipment from your own supplies or whether to hire elsewhere. If you have to hire equipment externally, the system alerts you if some of your own equipment of the same type becomes available, meaning you can end a costly hire early, saving money.

There are also great reports to see how money can be saved across the entire company. You get immediate access to actionable information on your equipment costs for every project, as well as information on loss, damage and maintenance costs. Knowledge is power, and this knowledge will dramatically reduce your costs on equipment and consumables.

This software is tailored to the exact requirements of your company, so for more information on Safety Agenda Plant and Asset Manager please email info@safetyagenda.com or call us on 020 7193 0835